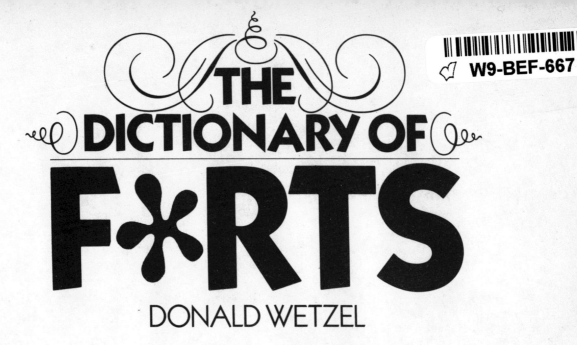

THE DICTIONARY OF F*RTS

DONALD WETZEL

CONTEMPORARY
BOOKS, INC.
CHICAGO

Published by Contemporary Books, Inc.
180 North Michigan Avenue, Chicago, Illinois 60601
Manufactured in the United States of America
International Standard Book Number: 0-8092-5124-8

Published simultaneously in Canada by Beaverbooks, Ltd.
195 Allstate Parkway, Valleywood Business Park
Markham, Ontario L3R 4T8 Canada

Introduction

To the best of my knowledge there has been no full length work attempted on the subject of farts. Which is hard to figure, as everyone on earth that lives and breathes also farts. Even the president. He farts oval farts. Due to the office. When my dad worked in an office he used to call it the orifice. I like puns but I do not think they belong in a book such as this. Otherwise I would have said that the president farts oval farts due to his orifice. Which would have been the best pun I ever thought of.

Note To Readers

All farts are divided into two groups:

1. Your farts
2. Somebody else's farts.

There are some farts that can only be positively identified when they are your own, such as the different kinds of silent or near silent farts. Odor alone will not always do. There is a feel to some farts that is necessary to their identification and naturally only the farter gets the feeling.

In case of doubt I will try and make clear which of the two groups each fart is apt to be found in. But the reader is asked to keep this in mind for himself when using this guide to avoid unnecessary confusion and false identifications.

All the farts in this book will be arranged alphabetically. If a person knows their alphabet they should have no trouble understanding this arrangement or figuring things out.

This is a good fart for the beginner. It is easy to identify. It starts with a loud unnaturally high note, wavers like a siren, and ends with a quick downward note that stops before you expect it to. It sounds like something is wrong. If it happens to you, you will know right off why it is called the Alarm Fart. You will be alarmed. The Alarm Fart, however, is rare.

The **Amplified Fart**

This is any fart that gets its power more from being amplified than from the fart itself. A metal porch swing will amplify a fart every time. So will a plywood table, an empty fifty gallon drum, a tin roof, or some empty cardboard boxes if they are strong enough to sit on. Any fart made a great deal louder than it really is through being amplified in this way can be called an Amplified Fart. These are common farts under the right conditions.

B

People who would never in their life know one fart from another, who would like to act like farts don't exist, will have to admit that a Bathtub Fart is something special.

It is the only fart you can see!

What you see is the bubble or bubbles.

The Bathtub Fart can be either single or multiple noted and fair or foul as to odor. It makes no difference. The farter's location is what does it.

Maybe there is a kind of muffled **pong** and one big bubble. Or there may be a **ping ping ping** and a bunch of bubbles.

The sound, I should point out, depends somewhat on the depth of the water and even more on the tub. If it is one of those big old heavy tubs with the funny legs you can get terrific sound effects. While one of the new thin ones half buried in the floor can be disappointing.

But either way, as long as the water is deep enough, whatever the sound, up comes the bubble or bubbles and you have to be quick—glance back over your shoulder and you have seen it, the Bathtub Fart, the most positively identifiable fart known to man.

It is a common fart and strictly group one unless you are a kid still young enough to take baths with your friends.

The Biggest Fart In The World Fart

Like the great bald eagle, this fart is pretty well described just by its name. This can either be a group one or a group two fart and can occur just about anywhere. I heard it one time, a group two identification, in a crowded high school auditorium one night, right in that silence that happens when a room full of people has stopped singing the Star-Spangled Banner and sat down. It came from the back. There was not a soul in that room that missed it. A fart like that can be impressive.

The most diagnostic characteristic of the Biggest Fart In The World is its size. Fart freaks who go around showing off, farting like popcorn machines and making faces before they fart or asking you to pull their finger and then they fart, never have what it takes for this one, which is rare even among your most serious farters.

The **Bullet Fart**

Its single and most pronounced diagnostic characteristic is its sound. It sounds like a rifle shot. The farter can be said to have snapped it off. It can startle spectators and farter alike. Fairly common following the eating of the more common fart foods, such as beans.

The **Burning Brakes Fart**

A silent fart identified by odor alone. Usually an adult fart, occurring while the adult is driving a car or has a front seat passenger who farts. The Burning Brakes Fart actually does smell a little like burning brakes and seems to hang around longer than most farts. Which gives whoever farted a chance to make a big show of checking to see if the emergency brake has been left on. When he finds it hasn't you know who farted. A common automobile fart.

The **Car Door Fart**

C

Either a group one or a group two fart.
Very tricky. It is meant to be a concealed
fart. A matter of close timing is involved,
the farter trying to fart at the exact
moment he slams the car door shut.
It is usually a good loud fart. It is one
of the funnier farts when it doesn't
work, which is almost every time.
It is a desperation fart and not
too common.

The **Celestial Fart**

Not to be confused with the Did An Angel Speak Fart, which is simply any loud fart in church. The Celestial Fart is soft and delicate, surprising in a boy or an adult. It is probably the most shy of all farts and might be compared with the wood thrush, a very shy bird. It does not have the sly or cunning sound of the Whisper Fart. It is just a very small clear fart with no odor at all. Very rare.

The **Chinese Firecracker Fart**

This is an exceptional multiple noted fart identified by the number and variety of its noises, mostly **pops** and **bangs**. Often when you think it is all over it still has a few **pops** and **bangs** to go. In friendly company, this one can get applause. Uncommon.

The **Command Fart**

This fart differs from the Anticipated Fart in that it can be held for long periods of time waiting for the right moment. Unlike the Anticipated Fart, it is intended to be noticed. A friend of mine, Harold Tabor, recently held a Command Fart for the whole period in Mrs. Schlotsheimer's history class and let it go right at the end, when she asked if there were any questions. Most well-timed public or private farts that work like this can safely be identified as Command Farts. Not too common.

The **Crowd Fart**

The Crowd Fart is distinguished by its very potent odor, strong enough to make quite a few people look around. The trick here is not to identify the fart but the farter. This is almost impossible unless the farter panics and starts a fit of coughing or starts staring at the ceiling or the sky as though something up there fascinates him. In which case he is the one. Very common.

The **Cushioned Fart**

A concealed fart, sometimes successful. The farter is usually on the fat side, sometimes a girl. They will squirm and push their butt way down into the cushions of a sofa or over-stuffed chair and ease out a fart very carefully without moving then or for some time after. Some odor may escape, but usually not much. Identification is difficult, and in doubtful cases should be listed as tentative. Common with some people.

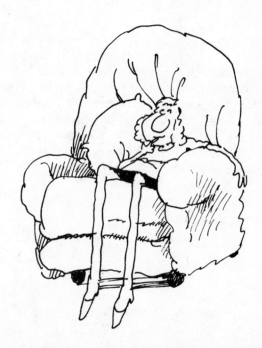

D

This is any loud fart in church. This fart was first called to my attention by my father. He probably read about it somewhere. For fart watchers who go to church, this is a good one to watch for as this is the only place it can be found.

The **Dog Did It Fart**

It is necessary for a dog to be around for this fart to occur. People who fart and blame it on the dog when there is no dog within miles are making a travesty of the whole fart identification business, which is difficult enough as it is. This is always a silent fart but one with an odor you could blame on a dog that was dead. The farter tries to blame it on the dog. He will even go so far as to run the dog out of the house. Do not be fooled. When a dog farts it will usually grunt too. It may even get up and walk away. This is what you should do when you have identified a Dog Did It Fart. They are vile.

The **Drum Roll Fart**

Some people might want to put this fart under the general heading of Musical Farts (see under **M**) but I for one have never considered the drum very much of a musical instrument. It is a multiple noted fart of the same tone or pitch farted very fast. It sounds more like a real drum roll when now and then the farter happens to throw in a rim shot at the end, but you cannot expect this every time. It should in no way be confused with the Chinese Firecracker Fart, which is by far the more colorful of the two, although the Drum Roll Fart is much more rare.

The **English Fart**

E

A very classy fart. The sound alone
distinguishes it from all other farts. There are
some who will say that this is a put-on accent,
but that is silly. When it comes to farting no
one goes around sounding like an Englishman. It happens or it doesn't. The sound it
makes is **thip.** Sometimes it will go **thip, thip.** It is unmistakable. It is probably as proper
and upper class as a fart can get.

The **Exclamation Fart**

This is a punctuation fart. Timing is the whole thing. The farter, or someone, must be speaking. For instance, the speaker will say, "Ah, shut up!" and then someone will fart a loud sharp fart. This is a true Exclamation Fart. If the speaker is also the farter he may delay his fart until the right moment and then force it for all he is worth. If it works it is still a true Exclamation Fart, although more often than not it is an accident and for this reason rare.

The Executive Fart

A very loud clear fart by a very
important person is an Executive Fart. It
is either sharp or flat, somewhat off key,
but otherwise a very businesslike fart.
No nonsense about it. But no one is supposed to notice. Particularly the farter. If you do
not laugh at the Executive Fart this is either because you are scared of the person who
farted or because the fart is so gross. Common with very important people.

There is probably no other fart about which there is more confusion or which has as many other common names. It has been called the Scorcher Fart, the Burning Britches Fart, the Solar Fart, the Natural Gas or Front Burner Fart, and other names. But its correct name is simply the Fire Fart. It is called this because of the sensation it gives the farter when he farts. It burns.

For this reason it is mostly a group one identification fart. People can make all kinds of faces when they fart. A look of pain when a person farts does not necessarily mean they have farted a Fire Fart. Some people look pained when they fart any kind of fart at all.

But as a group one fart there is never any question about it at all. You will wonder sometimes if it smokes. The only way this can be a group two identification is if it is confirmed. You have to say to the one who farted, "Did that fart burn?" If they say yes, you have identified and confirmed a group two identification Fire Fart. This will not happen very often.

The Fizzle Fart

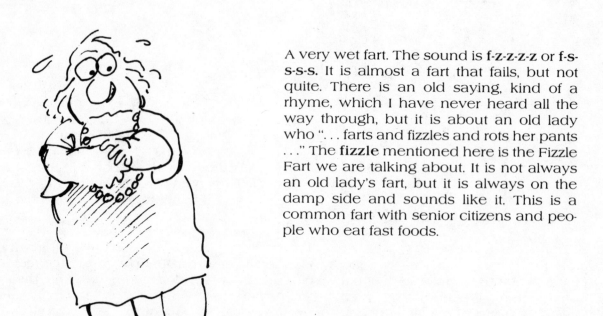

A very wet fart. The sound is **f-z-z-z-z** or **f-s-s-s-s**. It is almost a fart that fails, but not quite. There is an old saying, kind of a rhyme, which I have never heard all the way through, but it is about an old lady who ". . . farts and fizzles and rots her pants . . ." The **fizzle** mentioned here is the Fizzle Fart we are talking about. It is not always an old lady's fart, but it is always on the damp side and sounds like it. This is a common fart with senior citizens and people who eat fast foods.

The **French Fart**

Said to be the most beautiful of farts. Usually in a minor key. Soft and musical with many half-tones. Any long drawn out fart that seems beautiful to you is most likely a French Fart. Very rare.

The **G and L Fart**

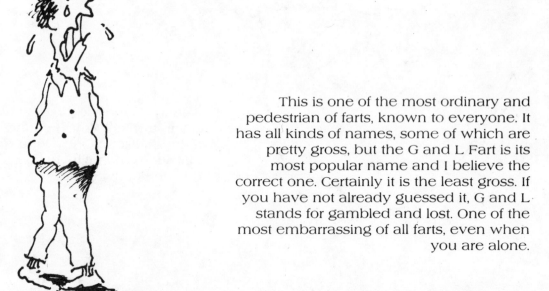

This is one of the most ordinary and pedestrian of farts, known to everyone. It has all kinds of names, some of which are pretty gross, but the G and L Fart is its most popular name and I believe the correct one. Certainly it is the least gross. If you have not already guessed it, G and L stands for gambled and lost. One of the most embarrassing of all farts, even when you are alone.

The **German Fart**

If you hear a fart that makes you think of a dog it is probably the German Fart. It has either a deep growling or a low barking noise, or both. It comes from deep inside and never seems to get all the way out. Still it can be loud and frightening to small children. The odor varies, but not much, as it is one of the rank ones every time.

The **Ghost Fart**

I consider the Ghost Fart a doubtful fart in most cases, as it is supposed to be identified by odor alone and to occur, for instance, in an empty house. You enter and smell a fart. Yet no one is there. People will insist that only a fart could have that odor, but I am of the opinion that it is just something that happens to smell like a fart. Maybe a dead rat. I have argued this with my friends and include the Ghost Fart here only at their insistence. However all identifications of the Ghost Fart should be listed as tentative or doubtful.

The **Girls Don't Fart Fart**

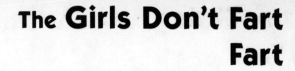

Any fart by a girl. A girl can fart a fart that will shake the walls or blow little birds right out of their nests, but the girl will never give a sign. You are supposed to ignore it. It may be hard to do, but you better do it. With girls this is the most common fart there is.

The **Going Up Stairs Fart**

A one in a million fart and one of my favorites. This fart breaks on each step as the farter goes up a short flight of steps. Not a step is missed when it is a true Going Up Stairs Fart. It is probably caused by being a held back fart and the action of going up some stairs cuts it loose. If the fart goes up a note with each step you have the Musical Going Up Stairs Fart. There is no fart more rare than this one.

The **Hair-Trigger Fart**

Another fart that hardly needs to be described. There is no one that lives and farts that does not know from experience what this fart is like. There is no sign it is on its way. Suddenly it is there. Just barely held back. Like a sneeze about to be sneezed. You know that any movement at all, even a thought, could set it off. And sure enough that is what will happen. A group one identification only. Very common.

The **Hard-Boiled Egg Fart**

Odor alone identifies this fart. It stinks of sulfur. Due to the sulfur content of hard-boiled eggs. While it is true that powdered sulfur will keep redbugs away when you are out in the woods it is not true that a few Hard-Boiled Egg Farts in the evening will keep a whole campsite free of redbugs for the rest of the night. What it may do is keep the campsite free of other campers for the rest of the night.

The **Harvard Fart**

The Harvard Fart is different from the English Fart in two ways. First, the sound is different. More of a **thap** sound than a **thip.** The other difference is the way the farter acts about it. With the English Fart, the farter always acts as though nothing has happened. But a person who farts a Harvard Fart will give a sign. He will smile. Or nod. As if he has just heard from God.

The Hic-Hachoo-Fart Fart

In my experience this is strictly an old lady's fart. What happens is unusual, but I have seen it once with an old lady playing cards with some friends and again with an entirely different old lady who had been bending over petting a cat and who did it as she stood up again. What happens is that the person manages to hiccough, sneeze, and fart all at the same time. The old lady that I saw do this playing cards, did it all—the whole thing; hic-hachoo-fart—before she could put down the card she was holding. That quick. After an old lady farts a Hic-Hachoo-Fart Fart she will usually pat her chest and say, "My, my," or "Well, well." There is no reason she should not be proud, as this is probably as neat an old person's fart as there is.

The **Incense Fart**

A potent fart. Do not be fooled by its name. It is only called the Incense Fart to be sarcastic. What happens is that someone farts in a crowd. A vile one. Since it cannot be ignored someone will say, "Ah, how lovely; Sandalwood? Jasmine? Gardenia?" Or whatever your favorite incense may be.

The **Inspirational Fart**

The sound of this fart may best be described as like organ music. However, in my opinion only someone really into farts would actually find this fart inspiring. Still, a sound like organ music is quite a fart, and if it actually gives you goose-flesh at the time it is probably safe to put it down as the Inspirational Fart. Rare.

The **Interrogatory Fart**

This is a fart that seems to ask a question. Ends on an up note. Seems to say, "Oh?" or "Well?" It can be a very silly fart when you are alone. As though you are having a conversation with your own ass. Fairly common.

The **Jerk Fart**

The Jerk Fart is a fart by a jerk, who smirks, smiles, grins, and points to himself in case you missed it. It is usually a single-noted, off-key, fading away, sort of whistle fart, altogether pitiful, but the jerk will act as if he has just farted the Biggest Fart In The World Fart. This should always be a group two identification.

J

The **John Fart**

I am talking here about the toilet john, not John as in John Brown or John Smith or someone you know named John. Start naming farts after your friends and the whole fart identification business will get altogether out of hand. The John Fart is simply any ordinary fart farted on the john. It is naturally a group one identification, with the sound, whatever it was, somewhat muffled. If that is all the person's trip to the john amounted to he will be disappointed for sure. Common as pigeons.

The **Jubilation Fart**

Generally the Jubilation Fart cannot be told safely from an Inspirational Fart except by an expert. Both farts are hard to believe. Like the hippopotamus and the rhinoceros. In the short time a fart lasts it is always hard to make up your mind which one it is. If you suddenly saw a hippopotamus or rhinoceros for as short a time you would probably have the same trouble. The rhinoceros is the one with the horn at the end of its nose.

The **Junk Fart**

This is a fart that we could just as well do without. It comes from eating junk and it sounds like it. A **pish-whish** sound. Like a swinging door. As farts go there is really nothing to it. It comes chiefly from eating at a fast food restaurant. It can happen while you are still there. Still eating. It's that quick. In and out, no waiting. The same as the service they advertise. This fart is way too common.

The **Kamikaze Fart**

Sometimes called the Suicide Fart or the Killer Fart. Kamikaze is the correct name. (Kamikaze means divine wind. For a fact.) It wipes out everybody. The farter in every case will have a crazy look about him. This is one of the ways this fart can be identified. The farter will be wiped out too. Any person who farts a Kamikaze Fart and brags about it is a fart fanatic and probably dangerous in other ways.

K

The **Kinky Fart**

A person who farts while kissing another person has farted a Kinky Fart. This is a rotten thing to do.

The **Kipling Fart**

The origin of this fart is interesting, if true.
It was supposed to have happened at the
University of South Alabama. What
happened was that a strange professor
was talking to another professor one day
who happened to be a great one for
making jokes and the strange professor said, "Do you like Kipling?" And the joker said, "I
don't know. How do you kiple?" And the strange professor said, "Like this." And then he
farted. This fart has a **kiple** sound.

The **Lead Fart**

The heaviest of all farts. It sounds like a dropped, ripe watermelon. Or a falling body in some cases. It is the only fart that goes **thud.** Except for the odor, which is also very heavy, it could be missed altogether as a fart. What was that? you might think. And never guess. Watch for this one. Rare.

The Loose Board Fart

The Loose Board Fart has to sound squeaky, like a loose board you have just stepped on. Some people call just any fart a Loose Board Fart. Just to have something to say. These are the same sort of people who say the dog did it when there is no dog in sight. Listen for the squeaky, creaky sound.

The Mud Sucker Fart

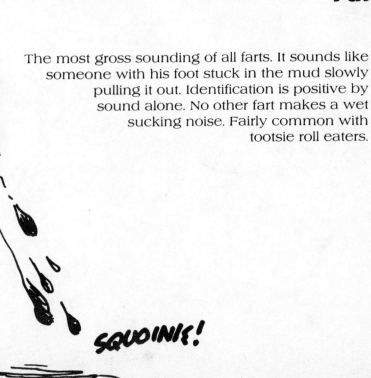

The most gross sounding of all farts. It sounds like someone with his foot stuck in the mud slowly pulling it out. Identification is positive by sound alone. No other fart makes a wet sucking noise. Fairly common with tootsie roll eaters.

SQUQINK!

The **Musical Fart**

This is a special category. All Musical Farts do not necessarily sound musical. This may seem odd, but that is the way it works. Who would think, for instance, that Spanish moss is related to the pineapple? But it is.

All Musical Farts are rare, and identification is often a matter of opinion.

The **Classical Fart**

Loud and soft, loud and soft. Goes on when you think it has ended

The **Hard Rock Fart**

A highly amplified musical fart. Can make a dog howl with pain. The farter doesn't care if you like it or not. You may not think it is musical but he does.

The **Star Spangled Banner Fart**

This is one of the few farts that can bring tears to people's eyes and lumps to their throats and otherwise get them all stirred up.

The **Wah-Wah Fart**

This is not a baby fart. The wah-wah is an electrical gadget worked by a guitar player's foot that makes an electric guitar make weird wah-wah sounds. Not all people would call this sound musical.

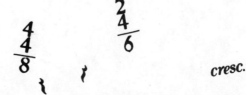

The **Natural Gas Fart**

N

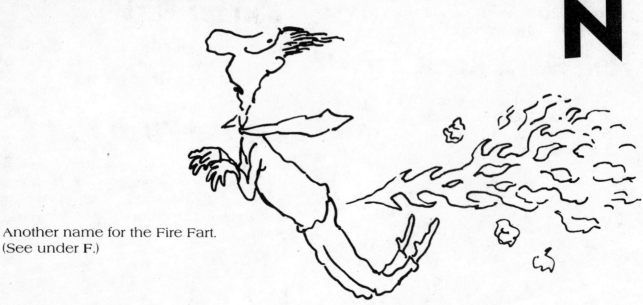

Another name for the Fire Fart.
(See under F.)

The **Octave Fart**

Some people would put the Octave Fart under Musical Farts. This would be a mistake but some will do it anyhow. All small birds that look like warblers are not warblers. Some are vireos. The Octave Fart goes under **O**. The sound of this fart is one note going up or down a full octave, quick or slow, loud or soft, major or minor. This may be a hard one to identify for a person who does not know what an octave is. Rare.

The **Organic Fart**

Sometimes called the Health Food Nut Fart.
Unless you are into health foods this will have
to be a group two identification. The person
who farts an Organic Fart may be talking about
the healthy food he eats even when he farts.
This makes identification easy. If he is heavily
into health foods he may even ask if
you noticed how good and pure and
healthy his fart smells. It may smell
to you like any other fart, but there
is no harm in agreeing with him. He
is doing what he thinks is best.

P

An unusual hollow sounding multiple-noted fart. Sound alone is diagnostic. It sounds like a ping-pong ball which has been dropped on a table from several feet up and then bounced until it fell off. There can be quite a wait between bounces. This is probably the most rare of all multiple-noted farts.

The **Poo-Poo Fart**

This is a fart by a very small kid. The kid farts
and then says, "Go poo-poo now." And
somebody takes him and he does.

The **President's Fart**

This rare fart was described in the introduction to this work. What is rare about this fart is that we are talking about presidents of the United States. There is only one of them at a time and they stay pretty much to themselves. But it is fair to suppose that they fart about as much as anybody else. Get one of these on your list, though, and you have really got one.

The **Quack-Quack Fart**

This is a silly name for a fart. A lot of people will call it the Duck Fart. But it is important to remember that this is a double-noted fart. And while **quack-quack** is the sound a duck makes and the sound of the Quack-Quack Fart, there is nothing to stop a duck from going quack just once, not twice. So that is why it is called the Quack-Quack Fart. Just to be exact. Fairly rare.

The **Quawonk Fart**

Somewhat similar to the Quack-Quack Fart. Mostly because of the **Q** sound. Very few farts have a **Q** sound. But the Quawonk Fart is single noted and far more soft and pleasant sounding than the Quack-Quack Fart. If you will say **quawonk** softly to yourself, that is the sound.

The **Rambling Phaduka Fart**

R

You must not be fooled by its pretty sounding name, as this is one of the most frightening of all farts. It is frightening to farter and spectator alike. It has a sound of pain to it. What is most diagnostic about it however is its length. It is the longest lasting fart there is. It will sometimes leave the farter unable to speak. As though he has had the wind knocked out of him. Spectators have been known to bite their knuckles bloody or even to faint while this fart is going on. A strong, loud, wavering fart, it goes on for at least fifteen seconds. If you are going to claim this one for your list you had better have witnesses, or there is a good chance people will say you have lied about it. Exceedingly rare.

The **Relief Fart**

The name should give you a pretty good idea about this particular fart. There are some farts that are a nuisance and some that are funny and some that are very peculiar, but the most popular fart of all is probably the Relief Fart. Sound or odor doesn't matter. What matters is the tremendous sense of relief that you have finally farted. This is usually a group one identification, but if the farter is the sort of person who is not afraid to show his feelings this can be a positive group two identification as well. Some people will even say, "Wow, what a relief." Very common.

The Rover Fart

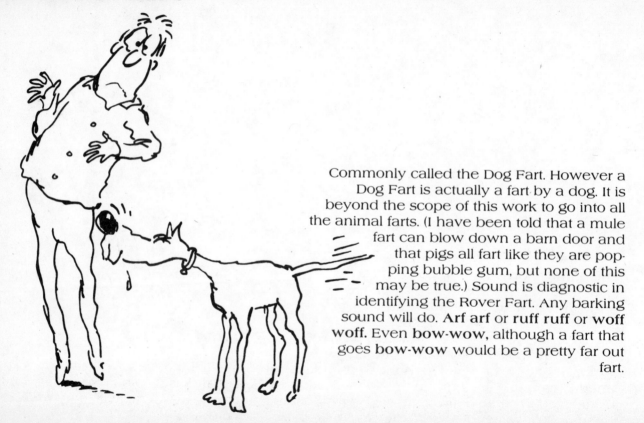

Commonly called the Dog Fart. However a Dog Fart is actually a fart by a dog. It is beyond the scope of this work to go into all the animal farts. (I have been told that a mule fart can blow down a barn door and that pigs all fart like they are popping bubble gum, but none of this may be true.) Sound is diagnostic in identifying the Rover Fart. Any barking sound will do. **Arf arf** or **ruff ruff** or **woff woff.** Even **bow-wow,** although a fart that goes **bow-wow** would be a pretty far out fart.

The **Rusty Gate Fart**

The sound of this fart seems almost impossible for a fart. It is the most dry and squeaky sound a fart can make. It sounds like the sound a blue jay makes when it is not crying **kat kat.** The Rusty Gate Fart sounds as if it would have worked a lot easier if it had been oiled. This fart is unknown to me as a group one identification, but it sounds like a fart that hurts.

The **S.B.D.** Fart

S.B.D. stands for **silent but deadly.** This is no doubt one of the most common farts that exists. No problem of identification with this one. Either group.

The **Scratchass Fart**

Surprisingly this is the only really dirty name for a fart in this whole work. But it is the right name all right. The action of the farter is diagnostic. He has farted and it itches. He just has to scratch. As a group two identification you have to make certain first that the person scratching his ass has really farted. Some people have a habit of scratching their ass about every five minutes. Common.

The S'cuse Me Fart

This rare fart excuses itself as it is farted. It is about as close to words as a fart can get. The sound it makes is like a little soft whisper that says, 'S'cuse me." The most polite of all farts and very silly when you are alone.

A truly awesome fart. It vibrates the farter.
Really shakes him up. People back away. It
sounds like an electric skillsaw ripping through a piece of half-inch
plywood. Very impressive. Not too common.

The Sonic Boom Fart

The people who believe in this fart claim that it is even bigger than the Biggest Fart In The World Fart. The Sonic Boom Fart is supposed to shake the house and rattle the windows. That is ridiculous. No fart in the world shakes houses and rattles windows. A fart that could do that would put the farter into orbit or blow his crazy head off.

The Sonic Boom Fart does not exist.

The **String of Pearls Fart**

A most unusual and perfect toned fart. Round clear evenly spaced notes. This one is really a beauty. Very rich ladies would like to fart this one every time if they could. Very rare.

The **Stutter Fart**

If you think stuttering is funny this is a very funny fart. It is a fart that can't seem to get going. The sound is best described as **pt, pt,pt-pt, pt-pt-pt, pop, pop-pop-pop-POW.** It is usually a forced-out fart that gets caught crossways as they say and only gets farted after considerable effort.

The Stutter Fart is not usually a funny fart to the farter. Rare.

The **Talking Fart**

T

This unusual fart sounds like it is imitating human speech. About the way a parrot does. Only the Talking Fart does not really say a thing. People will look at you and say, "What?" All you can do is shrug or look dumb.

The **Teflon Fart**

Slips out without a sound and no strain at all. A very good fart in situations where you would rather not fart at all. You can be talking to someone and not miss saying a word. If the wind is right he will never know. Unfortunately this is a rare fart unless the farter has been eating gumbo. Gumbo is a southern dish with a lot of okra in it.

The **Thank God I'm Alone Fart**

Everyone knows this rotten fart. You look around after you have farted and say, "Thank God I'm alone!" Then you get out of there. If it has to happen though, that is the best way for it to happen. Like finding out that your fly is unzipped. You should be alone.

The **Unmentionable Fart**

A tricky one to identify, even though it is probably more common than anyone wants to admit. It all depends on the situation or who farted. I will give some examples. You are alone with your girlfriend and she farts. Or you do. It may be loud or rank or both, but either way it is unmentionable. Or you are in the principal's office and there is just the principal and his secretary and you, and you didn't fart but somebody did. Much as you might like to say it wasn't you that did it, you know better. Either the principal or the secretary probably feels the same way. But the other one is very glad that the Unmentionable Fart cannot be mentioned. Or they would lose some Brownie points for sure.

The **Up-Tight Fart**

This is a kind of drawn-out Stutter Fart except that this one squeaks. Like a scared mouse. It takes an already naturally up-tight person to fart this fart. When he knows he has got to fart, like it or not, he gets even more up-tight. He may snap his sphincters shut like a steel trap, but out comes the fart. **Squeak, squeak, squeak.** It is embarrassing for everybody. Fairly rare, as people this up-tight generally stay to themselves most of the time anyhow.

The **Vending Machine Fart**

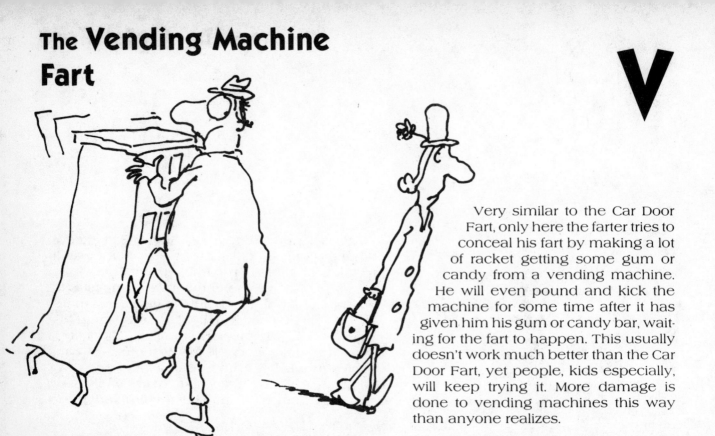

Very similar to the Car Door Fart, only here the farter tries to conceal his fart by making a lot of racket getting some gum or candy from a vending machine. He will even pound and kick the machine for some time after it has given him his gum or candy bar, waiting for the fart to happen. This usually doesn't work much better than the Car Door Fart, yet people, kids especially, will keep trying it. More damage is done to vending machines this way than anyone realizes.

The **Ventriloquist Fart**

This is something that just happens. Like an albino squirrel. It is doubtful if anyone can learn to throw his farts. But sometimes if all the conditions are right it will happen. And the person sitting next to the farter will look surprised and embarrassed and the farter will look surprised and pleased. This will have been a Ventriloquist Fart. This is an extremely hard one to identify unless you are the farter.

The **Volkswagen Fart**

Any good strong fart in a Volkswagen in the winter or anyhow with the windows closed is the deadly Volkswagen Fart. It can strangle people. While I am generally in favor of people farting whenever they have to fart, they really should try not to fart in a closed Volkswagen. It would be nice if this were one of the rare farts but it isn't.

W

The **Whisper Fart**

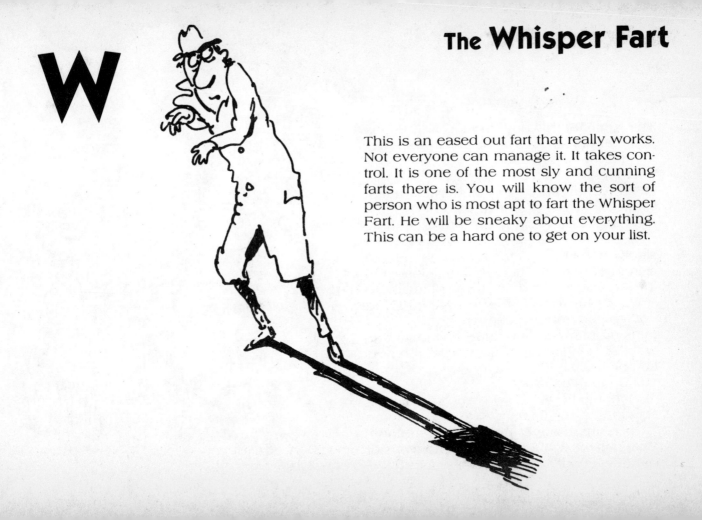

This is an eased out fart that really works. Not everyone can manage it. It takes control. It is one of the most sly and cunning farts there is. You will know the sort of person who is most apt to fart the Whisper Fart. He will be sneaky about everything. This can be a hard one to get on your list.

The Xmas Fart

The Xmas Fart is any ordinary fart that is farted at Christmas. That is the only special thing about it. That and the fact that it is a fart that starts with the letter **X**. An example of the Xmas Fart happened with me at school. It was not Christmas but the last day of school before Christmas. It happened in Mrs. Schlotsheimer's class. I was sitting at the back of the room right next to Harold Tabor, just the two of us alone. Being so close to Christmas I was sitting there singing Christmas carols in my head and not paying much attention and without thinking I farted a loud one. A regular firecracker. Heads turned all over the room as can be imagined.

I had to think fast.

"Hark the herald," I said. And I pointed at Harold.

Everyone thought that he was the one. Harold is crazy about puns but he was not so crazy about that one.

The **Yoga Fart**

This rare fart is a fart by a person sitting with their legs crossed thinking very heavy thoughts. The chance of a group two identification on this one is pretty slim, as who wants to hang around a person sitting with their legs crossed thinking very heavy thoughts. If it is a group one fart and you are really into Yoga then you should not even notice that you have farted. This could be a tough one to get on your list unless you or your friends are pretty weird.

The **Zipper Fart**

Z

This is the only fart that starts with the letter Z. It goes **Z-z-z-zip.** It hardly sounds like a fart at all. As a matter of fact there may not even be such a fart.

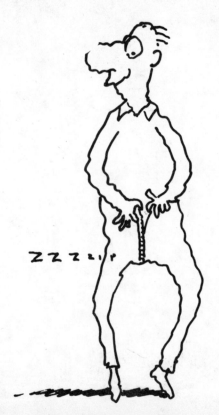

Z z z z z i p